GW00642659

something *South African* about *Food*

An introduction to South African Food and Wine by Glynn Orchin

phezulu
something about food

Something South African About Food

Enquiries should be addressed to:

Phezulu Independent Publishing
2-4 Main Street
Bangor
Northern Ireland
BT20 5AG

www.phezulu.co.uk

FIRST EDITION
APRIL 2010

ISBN: 978-0-9565560-0-4

Author: Glynn Orchin
Photography by Andrew Baird - Studio 82 Photography - www.art-id.co.uk
Design & Illustrations by Glynn Orchin & Richard Thompson - www.rickythompson.co.uk

Photos Supplied by:
pg 8: © www.rapideye.co.uk
pg 26 & 27: © Vivek Chugh, http://vivekchugh.blogspot.com
p 29 Cape of Good Hope; p 95 Lioness: © Nicolas Raymond
p29 Camps Bay: © John Maguire, www.sxc.hu
pg 92 & 93: © Michael Jung, www.sxc.hu
p97: Elephant Image: © Gil Ros www.sxc.hu
p85: Butternut Image: © www.picturepartners.nl
Front Cover: Peter Schwarz, www.peter-schwarz.de

Kind thanks to Nederburg Wines for suppling wine recommendations, information and images
Text and images pages 62 - 65 © Nederburg Wines Ltd. www.nederburg.co.za

Printed in Northern Ireland by W&G Baird Ltd.

Cooking & Recipe Information

All spoon measurements are level unless stated otherwise:

1 tsp	(teaspoon)	=	5ml	1oz	=	30g	
1 Tbl	(tablespoon)	=	15ml	2oz	=	60g	
¼ Cup		=	60ml	3oz	=	90g	
½ Cup		=	125ml	6oz	=	180g	
1 Cup		=	250ml	1lb	=	450g	

Oven Temperature Conversion

Gas Mark	Fahrenheit	Celsius
2	300	150
3	325	170
4	350	180
5	375	190
6	400	200
7	425	220

Pepper is freshly ground black pepper unless stated otherwise.

All recipes have been constructed to be suitably expanded or reduced to suit your dining requirements.

Preparation and cooking times are provided as guidelines. Oven cooking times relate to that of a fan-assisted oven, for conventional ovens increase the temperature by approximately 10°C. If you are unsure how accurate your oven is use an oven thermometer to verify the temperature.

Braai and barbeque cooking times will vary depending on the type of barbeque or braai you use ie. gas, charcoal or wood, will effect the cooking times.

Please ensure all dishes are cooked fully where applicable.

Braaivleis simply means 'roasted meat', commonly referred to as a braai it is the South African equivalent of the barbecue. More than just a traditional method of cooking meat, it is now growing in sophistication with marinades, spice rubs, breads and side dishes all being prepared over the open flames. The braai is a way of life for many South Africans as it encompasses their love for the outdoors with great food and great friends.

The braai logo identifies those that are suitable for braaing / barbecuing.

I recommend that you use fresh herbs, local produce, free range eggs/poultry wherever possible. As a conscientious chef I believe it is imperative that we take care of our environment and the world around us, when choosing ingredients please look for *Fairtrade*, organic and other ethically sourced / certified products.

Some images show an alternative method of presentation for recipes, images should be viewed as a guideline and not an exact representation of each recipe.

Contents:

Foreword

It is true to say that there is 'something about food' that intrigues and excites every one of us. Food is at the centre of our existence, we thrive on its depths of flavour and diversity to such an extent that we are constantly seeking new ways to engage and challenge our taste buds. 'something South African about food' will provide you with an insight into the stunning cuisine of South Africa so that you can experience the exciting culinary diversity that it has to offer. South Africa as a country may not have an extensive heritage of specifically defined dishes but what it does have in abundance is a fusion of international cuisine with local culture and tradition that is undeniably South African.

I was blessed to have been born in the extraordinary country that is South Africa, where from as early as I can remember I was introduced to the wealth of flavours and taste experiences that South Africa has to offer. From the simplest of Dutch style cooking to the complex marriage of flavours in Cape Malay cuisine I was fortunate to have access to this fusion of cultural cooking from a young age. From my early years living in Hillcrest outside of Durban to my frequent travels around the country, I have been privileged to have had first-hand experience of not only the wonderful food but also the excellent South African wines.

Now living in Northern Ireland I have, with great pride, established a South African influenced Restaurant, Phezulu Bistro, in the coastal town of Bangor, County Down. Through the restaurant I have aspired and strived to bring the British and Irish public an introduction to South African cuisine.

Proudly South African I believe that everyone should experience the breathtaking beauty and cultural diversity that South Africa has to offer. Based on my frequent journeys and culinary influences I have created this book to provide a simple introduction to South Africa and the cultural fusion of flavours. Beyond the food South Africa has earned itself a rightful place as one of the best wine producing countries on a global scale. With this success and achievement no winery has been more recognised and rewarded within South Africa than that of Nederburg.

As a chef I believe that great food should be prepared and served with wine that truly compliments and highlights the delicate flavours within each dish. I believe Nederburg to be among the very best of wine producers and have partnered with them in the development of this book to bring you an introduction to both Traditional and Contemporary South African Cuisine.

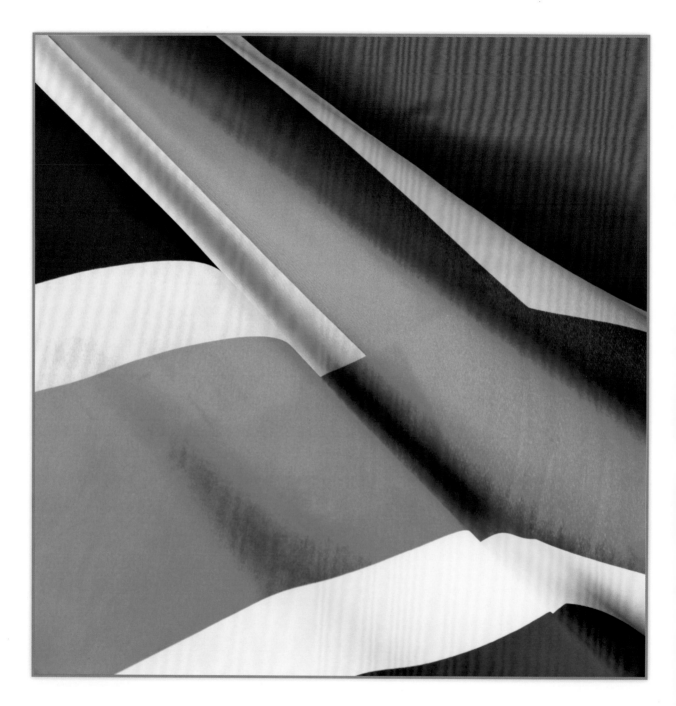

Introduction

South Africa as a country has had a colourful and dynamic emergence over the centuries. The abundance of natural resources not to mention the magnificent beauty encouraged nations from all over the world to colonise and settle within South Africa.

The first people to 'discover' South Africa were the Portuguese mariners who landed on the shores in the 15th century. Led by the explorer Bartolomeu Dias these sailors merely landed in South Africa to replenish their food reserves while on an expedition to discover a suitable trade route to India.

Despite this early discovery it was not until 1652 that the country was formally colonised by Europeans. This colony was first established by the Dutch East India Trading Company, the world's first multinational corporation. These Dutch settlers came with the sole intent of setting up a refreshment station in the area now known as Cape Town which was ideally situated along its spice trade route between the Netherlands and Asia. This 'Cape Colony' initially traded and bartered with the local indigenous people but eventually with the expansion of the colony the indigenous people found themselves without land. The Dutch East India Company encouraged more settlers to join the colony and along with these settlers came indentured workers from other countries such as India, Indonesia, Madagascar and Mozambique.

After conflict and power struggles between the French and British, the colony was captured in 1795 by the British who aimed to secure the valuable trade routes to Asia. This occupation by the British resulted in more European settlers being enticed to South Africa. Following years of growth and expansion by the British Empire the colony continued to grow and expand; with this expansion came a change in needs and desires of some of the settlers. The Voortrekkers, 'those who trek ahead', were Afrikaaners, Dutch in origin but born in South Africa and had developed their own culture and language which reflected their new African heritage. These pioneers travelled further afield into the wilderness to establish their own communities and eventually states when they became opposed to the policies and ideas being introduced and enforced by the British Empire on the colony.

Britain continued to expand its operations within South Africa and encouraged Europeans to migrate to South Africa. Over the centuries these settlers, including the British, Dutch, Italians, Portuguese, French Indians, and others all brought with them the traditions and culture of their homelands. This melting pot of culture and tradition has led to South Africa often being referred to as the 'Rainbow Nation'. The diverse culture combined with the stunning landscape has resulted in South Africa also being known as 'The World In One Country'

Following its 'rebirth' after the dark years of Apartheid, the 'New South Africa' has established itself as one of the world's top global travel destinations. From cosmopolitan cities to simple rural communities South Africa has an abundance of culture, choice and experience for everyone.

As a South African I am delighted to be able to provide you with recipe choices that represent and reflect some of the wonderful flavours from the Rainbow Nation of South Africa.

Starters & Soups

Butternut & Cinnamon Soup

5-6 people - preparation 15 minutes - cooking 30 - 35 minutes

This book would not do credit to South African Cuisine if it did not include a Butternut Soup recipe. Butternut Squash, similar to pumpkin is very versatile and lends itself perfectly to a number of cooking methods. In this recipe I have complimented the sweeter flavour by combining it with some typical Cape Malay ingredients.

2	medium onions - chopped		pinch	nutmeg
45g	butter		500g	butternut squash - peeled & chopped
3Tbl	cornflour		2Tbl	mango or apple chutney
1 tsp	curry powder (medium)		750ml	vegetable stock
1 tsp	ground cumin		750ml	milk
1 tsp	ground cinnamon			salt & pepper

- Saute the onions in the butter over a medium heat until translucent, 3 - 4mins.

- Mix cornflour, curry, cumin, cinnamon and nutmeg and stir into onions over a low heat.

- Add butternut and chutney, mix well over low heat and leave for 3 - 4mins, stirring occasionally.

- Pour in stock and milk, stir, cover and simmer for 15mins or until butternut is soft and tender, stirring occasionally.

- Remove any impurities from the surface with a spoon and liquidise the soup until smooth in texture. For extra smoothness pass through sieve.

- Season to taste.

Serve hot with fresh baked bread.

The flavour of this soup will develop further over 1 - 2 days so it is great for preparing in advance.

Roast Tomato & Chilli Soup

3-4 people - preparation 10 minutes - cooking 60 minutes

On a cold damp day there is nothing more comforting than a warm bowl of fresh tomato soup. This recipe with its chilli and garlic undertones and fresh herb garnish is sure to bring a warm glow.

7	ripe vine tomatoes		1 Tbl	brown sugar
1	medium red onion		½tsp	ground cumin
2	red bell peppers		2tsp	lemon juice
4Tbl	olive oil		pinch	cayenne pepper
3	garlic clove - minced			salt & pepper
700ml	chicken stock			basil or coriander
2Tbl	tomato paste			

- Cut the tomatoes and red onion in half and place onto a suitable baking tray.

- Cut the peppers into quarters, remove stalk and seeds and place on baking tray with tomatoes.

- Brush the surface of the tomatoes, peppers and onion with olive oil, sprinkle with garlic and season with salt and pepper.

- Place the tomatoes, peppers and onion in 180°C / 350°F preheated oven and bake for approximately 45 minutes. Tomatoes, peppers and onion may blacken a little around the edges.

- While the tomatoes, peppers and onion are cooking, combine the stock, tomato paste, sugar, cumin, lemon juice and cayenne in a food processor.

- Add cooked tomatoes, peppers and onion to the food processor and blend until smooth.

- Place the soup into a suitable saucepan and bring to the boil, reduce the heat and simmer for 10 - 12 minutes.

- Pass the soup through a sieve to remove seeds and skin, season to taste.

Serve hot with plenty of fresh chopped coriander or basil and fresh baked bread.

The flavour of this soup will develop further over 1 - 2 days so it is great for preparing in advance.

Sweet Potato & Thyme Soup

3-4 people - preparation 15 minutes - cooking 35 - 40 minutes

A popular South African Ingredient, sweet potato is an extremely useful vegetable that is great for frying, baking and stewing in a variety of different dishes. In this recipe I have combined it with a few other key ingredients to produce a smooth full bodied soup.

I	medium onion - chopped	400ml	vegetable stock
I Tbl	olive oil	300ml	milk
½	garlic clove - minced		salt & pepper
2	thyme sprigs		
400g	sweet potato - chopped		

- Saute onions in oil over high heat until translucent.

- Stir in garlic and thyme and reduce to low heat.

- Add sweet potato, stock and milk and simmer for 20 - 25 mins or until sweet potato is soft, stirring occasionally.

- Remove thyme and impurities from the surface with a spoon, liquidise the soup until smooth in texture.

- Pass through a sieve for extra smoothness.

- Season to taste.

Serve hot with fresh baked bread.

The flavour of this soup will develop further over 1 - 2 days so it is great for preparing in advance.

Chunky Oxtail Soup

4 people - preparation 20-30 minutes - cooking 3½ - 4 hours

Oxtail is an old South African favourite and is still very popular in many kitchens. The strong rich flavour of the meat and marrow provide a wonderful flavour base perfect for slow cooked soup or stews.

I	oxtail		3	bay leaves
3	medium onions - chopped		3	thyme sprigs
I	garlic clove - minced		I Tbl	tomato paste
4Tbl	olive oil		2litre	beef stock
250g	carrots - chopped			salt & pepper
250g	celery stalks - chopped			fresh parsley

- Trim excess fat from the oxtail and cut into equal sized sections 3 - 5 centimeters.

- Sauté the onions and garlic in oil over medium to high heat until translucent in a large saucepan.

- Add the oxtail and fry until golden brown all over.

- Reduce to medium heat, add carrots, celery, bay leaves, thyme and tomato paste - mix well.

- Pour over the beef stock, cover with a lid and simmer over a low heat for 3½ hours, stirring occasionally to prevent burning.

- Remove the oxtail, strip the meat from the bone and cut the meat into small pieces.

- Add the meat to the soup, season to taste.

Serve hot with fresh chopped parsley and fresh baked bread.

The flavour of this soup will develop further over I - 2 days so it is great for preparing in advance.

Wine Suggestion: *Cabernet / Merlot*

Roast Butternut Squash

2 people - preparation 10 minutes - cooking 45 - 55 minutes

This dish is based on a family favourite which simply combines three of South Africa's favourite ingredients. This version is a slight variation of the family recipe as I have opted to use butternut squash instead of gem squash since it is more readily available.

1	medium butternut squash - washed
2Tbl	olive oil
	salt & pepper
120g	creamed sweetcorn
60g	cheddar - grated

- Cut the butternut in half and remove the seeds.

- Brush the inside with olive oil and season.

- Place the butternut on a baking tray in 180°C / 350°F preheated oven and bake for 35 - 40minutes.

- Remove the butternut from the oven and fill with creamed sweetcorn and cover with a thick layer of cheddar, return to the oven for 10 - 12 minutes.

Serve hot as a starter or side dish.

Vegetable Samoosas

2 people - preparation 30-40 minutes - cooking 30 - 40 minutes

Originally from India these deep fried pastry parcels are usually filled with spicy vegetables or meats and are popular throughout South Africa. Samoosas are perfect for accompanying a main meal for eating as a light snack.

100g	potatoes - diced	¼tsp	ground turmeric
100g	carrot - finely chopped	½tsp	curry powder (medium)
100g	fresh peas	½tsp	ground - cumin
200ml	vegetable stock	½Tbl	lemon juice
1	medium onion - finely chopped	5g	coriander leaf - chopped
5g	butter	pinch	salt & pepper
2	green chillies - finely chopped (optional)		ready made filo pastry sheets
2	garlic cloves - minced		vegetable oil for frying
5g	fresh ginger - minced		

- Combine the potatoes, carrots, peas and stock in a small saucepan over low heat, cover and simmer until the liquid has evaporated, stirring occasionally to ensure the vegetables do not burn.

- Sauté the onion in the butter over a medium heat until translucent.

- Add the chillies, garlic, ginger, turmeric, curry, cumin and lemon juice to the onions and stir over low heat for 30 – 40 seconds.

- Combine the vegetables with the onions and mix well over low heat.

- Add the coriander, season to taste, remove from the heat and allow to cool.

- Thaw the pastry sheets, place one sheet on a clean smooth surface and cut into eight equal strips then brush 1 side with melted butter.

- Place a teaspoon of the filling slightly off centre to the left, approximately 1½ cm from the bottom edge.

- Fold the bottom edge up over the filling to form a triangle, continue to fold into triangles ensuring the corners are closed. Then brush with a little melted butter.

- Heat 5 - 6mm deep of oil over low to medium heat.

- Cook for 2 - 3 minutes each side or until golden brown.

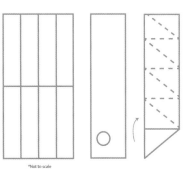

*Not to scale

Serve hot with your favourite chutney.

Peri Peri Chicken Wings

4 people - preparation 15 minutes (2h marinating) - cooking 20 - 45 minutes

Peri Peri or Piri Piri, simply means chilli chilli and was first introduced to South Africa as an essential cooking ingredient by Portuguese settlers.

24	fresh chicken wings
250ml	peri peri sauce see pg 91

- Place the chicken wings in a suitable mixing bowl, pour over the peri peri and mix well.

- Ensure the chicken is fully and evenly covered with the marinade and leave to infuse for between 2 and 24 hours, turning occasionally.

- These wings are great for braaing / barbecuing, cook over suitable coals for 20 - 25 minutes or until golden brown and juices run clear.

Alternatively

- When the weather is poor the oven is just as good, place on a greased baking tray and cook in 180°C / 350°F preheated oven for 40 - 45 minutes or until golden brown and juices run clear.

Serve hot with fresh leaf salad and extra dipping sauce.

These wings are also ideal for eating cold as a snack or part of a picnic.

Cape Town, South Africa

Cape Town, 'The Mother City'

Cape Town also known as the 'Mother City' was first founded in 1652 by the Dutch East India Company who chose it as a suitable refreshment station on its sailing route between the Netherlands and Asia. The Dutch influence on the region can be observed in the style, culture and architecture of the city and surrounding areas while the latter British and Cape Malay influences can also be observed in the diverse culture and cuisine. Cape Town is an ever popular tourist destination for visitors from all over the world and has an abundance of stunning attractions such as the dramatic Table Mountain, Victoria and Alfred Waterfront, Robben Island, and the surrounding areas such as Stellenbosch, Simon's Town and of course Nederburg winery.

Table Mountain, the most popular of the attractions, towers over the city creating an impressive backdrop to the city skyline and Table Bay harbour. Table Mountain is part of the Cape Peninsula Mountain Chain which stretches from the North of Cape Town to the southern Cape of Good Hope and Cape Point.

If you enjoy a scenic hike there are fantastic walking routes up to the top of the mountain, for those who have less time there is a modern cable car with a revolving floor that offers a wonderful vantage point to take in the beauty of both the city bowl and the mountain itself. Along the coastal 'Garden Route' you can take in the beauty of the Cliffs, beaches and of course the abundance of plant life including the national flower, the Protea.

Robben Island or Seal Island is located seven kilometres off the coast of Cape Town where Nelson Mandela was imprisoned during the time of apartheid before his release and subsequent rise to fame as South Africas' first democratic black president. Robben Island is now a World Heritage Site and museum showcasing the history of the Island and South Africa.

Simon's Town is located on the eastern side of The Cape peninsula and has been an important harbour and naval base for over two centuries. One of Simon's Towns attractions is Boulders beach, as the name implies it is a beach with what can only be described as having huge boulders strewn across the sand. This in itself is a sight to be seen but the real fascination with the beach lies in its natural colony of African Jackass penguins. These endangered little penguins enjoy their day swimming in the waters of False Bay and sunning themselves on the white sands of Boulders Beach.

Stellenbosch located to the east of Cape Town was the second European settlement to be established after Cape Town. The style and architecture of the town is typically Dutch with decorative white washed buildings and cobbled streets. Today it is the home to Stellenbosch University and an array of successful wineries not to mention stylish restaurants, boutique hotels and fashionable shops. This is a great place to visit and is always on my list of things to do when in Cape Town.

Cape Town's natural beauty is apparent from the first moment you lay your eyes on Table Mountain but I find the best way to take it all in is to take a boat trip out from the harbour. A tremendous number of businesses operate out of the waterfront offering a range of services from trips to Robben Island to whale watching along the coast. Of course if you prefer something more 'challenging' some of these boat tour companies offer the ultimate Great White shark cage diving experiences.

Whichever of these trips you choose you will be guaranteed the most amazing view of the City, Table Mountain and the Twelve Apostles, the twelve peaks that run along the coast from Table Mountain. Be sure to check out the sea conditions before booking your boat tickets as the waves can get pretty rough. Unfortunately I speak from experience.

Cape Town is one of my favourite places to visit and never fails in its offerings.

Main Courses & Entrees

Pork Fillet & Plum Sauce

4 people - preparation 10 - 15 minutes - cooking 15 - 20 minutes

As a child I remember having to be patient and wait for what seemed forever to pick the ripest plum from our tree in the back garden. Fortunately nowadays I just have to pop into a local shop to pick up juicy ripe South African plums.

2	pork fillet - trimmed		**Plum Sauce**	
	salt & pepper		20g	butter
			6	ripe purple or red plums - sliced
25g	butter		60ml	red wine
	fresh rosemary		80g	brown sugar
			1 Tbl	honey
			3 Tbl	tomato paste
			2 Tbl	Worcestershire sauce
			1 Tbl	lemon juice

- Cut the pork fillet into 2 ½ cm / 1 inch thick medallions and season.

- In a large frying pan or skillet heat the butter over high heat until it foams, add the medallions and reduce to medium heat, cook medallions on each side for 8 - 10 minutes or until cooked throughout.

- Remove the medallions from the heat, make a small incision in the centre and insert a small sprig of rosemary in each medallion.

Plum Sauce

- Heat the butter in a small saucepan over medium heat.

- Add the plums and cook for 2-3minutes, add red wine, brown sugar, honey, tomato paste, Worcestershire sauce and lemon juice, mix well.

- Simmer for 3-4 minutes stirring occasionally, season if required.

Serve with roast potatoes and steamed vegetables.

Braai Style Ribs

4 people - preparation 20 minutes - cooking 2¼ hours

The Braai or "Barbeque" is definitely South Africa's favourite method of cooking. This recipe incorporates a typical Braai style marinade with spare pork ribs.

1kg	pork ribs		1	garlic clove - minced
2Tbl	honey		1 tsp	Dijon mustard
30ml	olive oil		1 Tbl	chutney
30ml	white wine		pinch	ground cumin
20ml	Worcestershire sauce		pinch	ground coriander
2Tbl	tomato paste		pinch	salt & pepper
1 Tbl	brown sugar			

- Place ribs in a mixing bowl

- Combine the other ingredients in a blender and blend until smooth.

- Pour sauce over the ribs and marinate between 2 and 24 hours.

- Place the ribs on a suitable baking tray and place uncovered in preheated 170°C / 325°F oven and cook for 30minutes.

- Remove from the oven and pour off any excess oil / liquid. Turn the ribs and baste with the remaining braai sauce. Return to the oven and cook for 1 hour and 45 minutes.

- Remove from the oven.

Serve hot with fresh salad. See pg 87.

Boerewors

7 people - preparation 25 minutes - cooking 15 - 20 minutes

Boerewors or Farmer's Sausage is as traditional as it comes. These aromatic and flavoursome sausages are a staple dish throughout South Africa, combining the beef and pork with aromatic spices.
I recommend you speak to your local butcher to prepare this recipe.

20g	coriander seeds		5g	pepper
700g	beef - minced coarsely		1 tsp	ground nutmeg
700g	pork - minced coarsely		1 tsp	ground allspice
100g	pork fat - minced (spek)		40ml	malt vinegar
3	garlic cloves - minced		20ml	Worcestershire sauce
15g	salt		50g	sausage casing

- Toast the coriander seeds in a pan over high heat, cool and grind the seeds.

- In a separate bowl combine the beef, pork and spek in a mixing bowl.

- Add coriander, garlic, salt, pepper, nutmeg and allspice.

- Mix in the vinegar and Worcestershire sauce.

- Leave to infuse for 30 minutes.

- Pack the meat into the sausage cases, not too tight or else they will split when cooking.

- Boerewors are best cooked on a braai / barbecue for 15 - 20 minutes, turning occasionally.

Alternatively:

- Pan fry in oil and butter for 15 - 20 minutes, turning occasionally.

Serve with salad see pg 87, chutney or chakalaka see pg 84.

Beef Fillet & Pinotage Jus

4 people - preparation 15 minutes - cooking 10 - 15 minutes

Well balanced with plum and cherry aromas Pinotage is a uniquely South African red wine and was first developed by Abraham Izak Perold in 1924. The rich flavour of the jus compliments the gentle flavour of the beef fillet, this recipe can also be prepared with stronger exotic game meats such as Zebra, Springbok or Impala.

4	beef fillet 225g / 8oz each
2	garlic clove - minced
	salt & cracked black pepper
3Tbl	olive oil
2Tbl	butter
160g	baby spinach
2Tbl	water

Pinotage Jus

3Tbl	butter
2	shallots - finely chopped
120ml	pinotage (red wine)
2	sprigs rosemary
2	sprigs thyme
240ml	beef stock
½tsp	caster sugar

- Bring the steaks to room temperature before cooking.
- Remove excess moisture from the fillets with kitchen paper, rub the garlic into the beef then season generously.
- Heat the olive oil in a large heavy bottomed frying pan/skillet over high heat, once hot add the butter and the fillets, sear for 3 - 4 minutes, then turn and sear for a further 3-4 minutes or until both sides are browned. Sear the edges of the fillets until evenly browned. Reduce to a medium to low heat and continue to cook turning occasionally until fillets are cooked to your liking.

rare:	total cooking time of: 8-10	minutes
medium rare:	total cooking time of: 10-12	minutes
medium:	total cooking time of: 12-14	minutes

Red Wine Jus

- In a small saucepan melt 2Tbl butter, add the shallots, and cook for 2 - 3 minutes or until translucent.
- Add the pinotage wine, rosemary and thyme, bring to the boil and continue to boil until most of the wine has evaporated then add stock and sugar, stir to melt sugar, simmer for 3 - 4 minutes over low heat.
- Optional: for a smooth finish strain the sauce to remove the shallots, thyme and rosemary.
- Bring the sauce to the boil and continue boiling until the sauce thickens enough to evenly coat the back of a spoon.
- Add the remaining butter and melt just before serving to give the sauce a rich glossy finish.

Wilted spinach

- Rinse the spinach leaves with clean water and strain to remove excess liquid.
- Heat 2T water in a small saucepan over low heat, add the spinach and cover with lid, simmer for 2-3 minutes or until spinach has wilted.

Serve with butternut mash see pg 85 or roast vegetables.

Bunny Chow

4 - 6 people - preparation 15 minutes - cooking 60 minutes

It is commonly believed that the Bunny Chow was introduced to South Africa in the 1940's by an Indian restaurant owner in Durban. To work around apartheid laws that excluded black people from dining in his restaurant the owner is said to have sold his curry through a hatch onto the street. However the traditional roti bread was by no means an ideal vessel for the curry, thus the idea to serve the curry in a hollowed out loaf of bread was introduced. Indian shopkeepers around Grey's Street were known as Banias or Banyas. This Banya food or chow over time became more commonly known as Bunny Chow and has thrived across South Africa ever since

½tsp	ground cinnamon	I tsp	ginger - minced
¼ tsp	nutmeg - grated	2	chillis - chopped
I tsp	ground paprika	I Tbl	lemon juice
3tsp	garam masala curry powder	75g	mild chutney
½tsp	ground turmeric	I tsp	sugar brown
I ½tsp	ground cumin	2	bay leaves
½tsp	salt	400g	tomatoes - chopped
½tsp	pepper	300ml	stock
4Tbl	canola oil or olive oil	I	green bell pepper - chopped
2	medium onion - chopped	2	small loaves bread un-sliced
750g	rump beef - cubed		fresh coriander
2	garlic cloves - minced		

- Combine the cinnamon, nutmeg, paprika, curry, turmeric, cumin salt and pepper.
- Heat a small pan over high heat and add the spice mix, heat for I - 2 minutes to lightly toast the spices.
- Remove spices from the heat and set aside.
- Heat a medium sized saucepan over high heat and add the canola oil, onions and beef, cook until beef is evenly browned all over and the onions are translucent.
- Reduce to medium heat and add garlic, ginger, chillis and lemon juice, stir well.
- Reduce to low heat and add the toasted spices, chutney, sugar, bay leaves and tomatoes, stir well.
- Pour in the stock , stir and cover with a lid, allow to cook for 45 - 60 minutes, stirring occasionally.
- Add the green bell pepper, cover and cook for a further I5 minutes.
- Cut the bread loaves in the middle and carefully hollow out to form 'bread bowls'. Do not throw away the inside of the loaves as this is great for eating with the curry.

Serve the curry in the 'bread bowls'
garnished with plenty of fresh coriander and sambals see pg 88.

Frikkadels & Monkey Gland Sauce

2-4 people - preparation 30 minutes (2hrs marinating) - cooking 6 - 12 minutes

No Monkeys were harmed in the making of this sauce. Despite the unusual name this sauce actually has nothing to do with Monkeys. It is commonly believed the sauce was originally developed by frustrated French chefs in South Africa who could not understand the cultural tastes of South Africans. The chefs out of spite, simply combined a variety of random ingredients to make a 'sauce'; inadvertently they created the now very popular Monkey Gland Sauce.

500g	mince beef
1	medium onion - finely chopped
40g	breadcrumbs
1 Tbl	red wine
½ tsp	coriander seeds - toasted & crushed
¼ tsp	ground nutmeg
1 tsp	salt
½ tsp	pepper
1	egg
	sunflower oil (for frying)

Monkey Gland Sauce

2	onions - chopped
1	garlic clove - minced
2 Tbl	olive oil
50ml	red wine
2	tomatoes - chopped
100ml	mild chutney
100ml	tomato paste
50ml	beef stock
50ml	Worcestershire sauce
1 Tbl	Dijon mustard
	salt & pepper

- Mix together the beef, onion, breadcrumbs, red wine, coriander, nutmeg, salt and pepper.

- Whisk the egg and add it to the mix.

- Ensure mixture is thoroughly mixed and divide into 12 equally sized balls.

- Slightly flatten the balls and lightly cook them in the oil until browned 10 - 15 minutes; or until cooked.

Monkey Gland Sauce *(also great with steaks, chicken and lamb)*

- Sauté the onions and garlic in the oil.

- Add red wine and simmer for 2 - 3 minutes to cook off the alcohol.

- Stir in tomatoes, chutney, tomato paste, beef stock, Worcestershire sauce and mustard and simmer for 5 minutes.

- Season to taste.

Serve hot with basmati rice or pasta.

Bobotie

4-6 people - preparation 15 minutes - cooking 30 - 35 minutes

This is one of South Africa's most popular dishes. It was most probably introduced by Dutch settlers in the 17th century but most definitely influenced by the Cape Malay / Muslim community.
Originally made with mutton it lends itself very well to lamb, beef, pork and vegetables.

2	medium onions - chopped	½tsp	ground cinnamon
3Tbl	olive oil	1 Tbl	salt
1kg	lean minced beef (or meat of your choice)	½tsp	pepper
3	garlic gloves - minced	2 slices	thick cut bread (no crusts)
4Tbl	chutney	200ml	milk
1 Tbl	curry powder (medium)	4	medium eggs
1 Tbl	ground paprika	50g	raisins
1 Tbl	ground cumin	3	bay leaves

- Saute the onions in the olive oil over a medium heat until translucent.

- Add the meat and fry over medium heat until lightly cooked and crumbly.

- Reduce to low heat, add garlic, chutney,curry, paprika, cumin, cinnamon, salt and pepper, mix well and remove from heat.

- Soak the bread in milk for 2 - 3 minutes, squeeze bread and retain left over milk. Use a fork to break up the bread and mix it into the meat.

- Beat two of the eggs and mix into the meat along with the raisins

- Spoon the mixture into a greased baking dish and place into a preheated oven at 180°C / 350°F for 15 - 20minutes

- Beat two eggs into the leftover milk, season and pour over the meat, garnish with bay leaves and return to the oven for 25 - 30minutes

Serve hot with chutney and yellow rice, see pg 86.

Boerie Burger

6 people - preparation 10 minutes - cooking 15 - 20 minutes

This recipe is based on the ever popular Boerewors or 'Farmer's Sausage' recipe using some of the key ingredients. It makes a fantastic Gourmet beef burger full of flavour.

14g	coriander seeds	¼ tsp	pepper
1kg	lean beef - minced	¼ tsp	ground allspice
2	garlic cloves - minced	5g	salt
20ml	malt vinegar		olive oil for frying
15ml	water	6	ciabatta or floury rolls
¼ tsp	gorund nutmeg		

- Toast the coriander seeds in a pan over high heat, cool and grind the seeds.

- Place the mince into a suitable mixing bowl.

- Mix the coriander, garlic, vinegar, water, nutmeg, pepper, allspice, salt and oil, combine with mince.

- Mix well and divide into six evenly sized balls.

- Press and mould the balls into flat discs approximately 9 - 10cms wide.

- Pan fry in a little oil over a medium to low heat for 15 - 20 minutes, turning occasionally.

- Braai/barbecue time 15 - 20 minutes or until cooked throughout, turning occasionally.

Serve in a warm ciabatta or soft floury roll with
dressed salad and chutney or Monkey Gland sauce see pg 43.

Apricot Lamb Sosaties

2 people - preparation 15 minutes - cooking 8 - 15 minutes

Sosaties or kebabs are a perfect addition to any Braai. These sosaties balance the sweet flavour of the apricots against the gentle flavour of the lamb with a subtle hint of curry.

400g	lamb - cubed
4	wooden kebab skewers
16	apricots - dried
1	red bell pepper
1	green bell pepper

Apricot Glaze

1	sprig rosemary
½	garlic clove - minced
1 tsp	wholegrain mustard
¼ tsp	curry powder (medium)
1 tsp	vinegar
3 Tbl	apricot preserves
1 Tbl	olive oil
	salt & pepper

- Place the lamb in a suitable dish and pour over the apricot glaze, ensuring the lamb is evenly coated. Leave to marinate for at between 2 and 24 hours.
- Soak the kebab skewers in water for 30 minutes to prevent them burning.
- Skewer the lamb, peppers and apricots and place back in the marinade.
- Cook the sosaties over suitable coals or grill for 10 – 15 minutes or until cooked to your liking, turn often.

Apricot Glaze
- Pick the rosemary leaves and place in a mortar add the garlic, mustard, curry and pound together.
- Mix in the vinegar, apricot preserves, olive oil and a pinch of salt and pepper.
- Combine all the ingredients in a small pot and melt together over low heat for 1-2 minutes

Serve with salad see pg87 or yellow rice see pg86

Lamb Tamatie Bredie

2 people - preparation 20 minutes - cooking 3 hours

This was traditionally a slow cooked tomato and mutton stew and is a well established South African dish. However modern times have led to other meat such as lamb and beef being substituted for the mutton. My personal variation for this dish is to oven cook the stew using lamb shanks as this gives the dish excellent flavour and nice presentation potential.

4Tbl	butter		1 tsp	cornflour
2	lamb shanks		1 Tbl	chutney (mild)
1½	medium onions - sliced		1 Tbl	Worcestershire sauce
2	garlic cloves - minced		1 tsp	lemon juice
1 tsp	ground paprika		60g	tomato paste
P	chilli powder		4	tomatoes - chopped
½ tsp	marjoram - dried		1	potato, peeled - chopped
2	cardamon seeds		2tsp	thyme
2Tbl	red wine		300ml	stock, lamb, beef or chicken
1 tsp	brown sugar			salt & pepper

- Melt the butter in a large oven suitable pot over high heat add the two shanks and brown evenly, remove the lamb and set aside

- Saute the onions in the remaining butter until lightly browned; stir in garlic, paprika, chilli, marjoram, cardamom seeds and red wine, reduce to a medium to low heat.

- Add the sugar, cornflour, chutney, Worcestershire sauce and lemon juice, mix well.

- Mix in the tomato paste then add the tomatoes, potato, thyme and stock.

- Season the lamb with salt and pepper and place into the pot with the sauce, cover with a lid and place in 180°C / 350°F preheated oven cook for 2½ – 3 hours or until meat is tender and falls from the bone.

- Season to taste

Serve hot from the oven with fresh baked bread, garnish with chopped thyme or rosemary.

Aromatic Lamb Cutlets & apricot gastrique

2 people - preparation 10 minutes - cooking 20 minutes

Lamb dishes are popular throughout all of Africa. This dish delicately balances the distinct lamb flavour with a medley of mild spices to bring out the best in Cape Malay flavours.

4	lamb cutlets	**Apricot Gastrique**	
2tsp	ground cumin	250g	apricots - peeled & chopped
	salt & pepper	15g	butter
¼	garlic clove - minced	125ml	white wine vinegar or white vinegar
2Tbl	olive oil	75g	caster sugar
		¼	garlic clove - minced
		¼ tsp	salt

- On one side of the cutlets sprinkle over half the cumin followed by salt and pepper - rub the cumin and half the garlic into the meat ensuring an even coating.

- Turn over the cutlets and repeat on the other side.

- Heat the olive oil in a frying pan over high heat. Place the cutlets in the pan and turn down to low to medium heat, cover with a lid and cook for 2 - 3 minutes. Turn the cutlets and cook for a further 3 - 4 minutes or until cooked to your liking.

Apricot Gastrique

- Combine all the sauce ingredients in a saucepan and bring to the boil.

- Reduce to low heat and simmer for 15 - 20 minutes or until fruit is soft and tender.

- Blend until smooth.

- Season to taste.

Serve with spiced cous cous.

Venison Potjiekos

6 - 8 people - preparation 20 - 30 minutes - cooking 3 Hours

Potjiekos or "pot food" is traditonally the slow cooking of meat and vegetables in a cast iron pot over hot coals. Nowadays not much has changed with this cooking method except for the increased variety of ingredients. Most South Africans will have their own Potjie, not to mention a well guarded family recipe.

3Tbl	olive oil		½tsp	ground allspice
3	medium onions - sliced		4	tomatoes - chopped
2	garlic cloves - minced		½tsp	salt
200g	bacon finely - chopped		½tsp	pepper
1kg	venison or beef - cubed		6	medium potatoes - cubed
1Tbl	tomato paste		4	carrots - diced
1Tbl	thyme leaves		500g	grated or finely sliced cabbage
1tsp	curry powder (mild)		250ml	red wine
1tsp	ground paprika		250ml	beef stock

- Heat olive oil over high heat in a Potjie or heavy bottomed saucepan.

- Add the onions, garlic, bacon and venison and cook for 5 - 6 minutes or until the meat is browned all over.

- Stir in the tomato paste, thyme, curry, paprika, allspice, tomatoes, salt and pepper, reduce to low heat.

- Layer the potatoes on top of the meat mixture, followed by a layer of carrots then a layer of cabbage, do not stir.

- Combine the red wine and stock and pour over the top.

- Cover with a lid and cook for three hours, do not stir.

- Stir and check seasoning.

Serve with fresh crusty bread or rice.

This flavour in this dish will develop further over 1 - 2 days.

Mango Chilli Salmon

2 people - preparation 15 minutes - cooking 10 - 15 minutes

Throughout South Africa you will find a wonderful amount of fresh fish restaurants all showcasing the complex marriage of flavour with South Africa's love of seafood. This contemporary dish infuses the spicy and the sweet flavours with the full flavour of salmon and mussels

2	6oz salmon fillets		**For the sauce:**	
	salt & pepper		10g	butter
2Tbl	olive oil		200ml	double cream
300g	fresh mussels		2T	mango chutney
			½tsp	chilli flakes
			pinch	ground turmeric
			¼	garlic clove - minced
				salt & pepper

- Season the salmon fillets.

- Heat the olive oil in a frying pan over high heat and place the salmon skin side down into the pan, sear for 3 - 4 minutes, turn and cook for 2 - 3 minutes.

- Remove from the heat and place the salmon on a suitable baking tray, place in 180°C / 350°F preheated oven and cook for 4 - 5 minutes.

- Scrub the mussels in fresh water, remove any beards and discard those with broken or cracked shells or that do not close when firmly tapped.

For the Sauce

- In small heavy bottomed saucepan combine half the butter with the cream, chutney, chilli flakes, turmeric and garlic and heat over a low to medium heat for 1 - 2 minutes stirring occasionally.

- Add the mussels and cover with a lid and simmer for 5 minutes to allow the mussels to steam cook, uncover and stir the mussels. Cover for a further 5 minutes or until the vast majority of the mussels have opened. Discard any mussels that have not opened as they are not suitable for consumption.

- Add the remaining butter, melt and serve.

- Alternatively you can simply steam the mussels in water and prepare the sauce separately.

Serve with potatoes, rice, salad or cous cous.

Hake & Sundried Tomato Pesto

2 people - preparation 10 minutes - cooking 10 - 15 minutes

With similar climates it is not hard to imagine how the Mediterranean has influenced South African cuisine. The deep flavour of the tomatoes infused with the fresh fragrant basil compliments the mild taste of Hake.

2	Hake Fillets, skin on		*Pesto*	
	salt & pepper		200g	semi sundried tomatoes in oil
3Tbl	flour		20g	parmesan - grated
3Tbl	olive oil		80ml	olive oil
			70g	pine nuts or similar
			1	garlic clove - minced

- Combine all the pesto ingredients and blend until smooth.

- Score the skin side of the hake fillets and season with salt and pepper and coat with flour.

- Heat the olive oil in a skillet or frying pan over high heat. When hot place the hake into the pan skin side down and sear for 2 - 3 minutes turn and sear for 1 - 2 minutes.

- Remove from the plan and place on a suitable baking tray skin side up.

- Spoon the pesto evenly onto the hake, place in 180°C / 350°F preheated oven and cook for 6 - 8 minutes or until flesh is firm.

    Serve with crushed herb potatoes and green beans, rice or salad see pg 87.

Lemon Pepper Cod

2 people - preparation 10 minutes - cooking 15 - 20 minutes

This Dish brings together South Africa's love for fish and air cured meat. Their passion for combining the Italian influences with South African grown lemons creates a delightful taste experience.

2	cod fillets (6oz each)
	salt & pepper
4	slices parma ham

Lemon sauce

200ml	double cream
2Tbl	lemon juice
2tsp	lemon pepper spice
1/4tsp	crushed black pepper
½	garlic clove - minced
5g	butter

- Season the cod fillets

- On a sheet of grease proof paper 21cm x 21cm place two slices of parma ham overlapping to fit the size of the cod fillet.

- Place the cod fillet on the parma ham and use the greaseproof paper to roll the parma around the cod, ensuring the paper does not get trapped. Skewer with two or three cocktail sticks to secure the Parma ham.

- Place the cod parcels onto a greased baking tray and place in 180°C / 350°F preheated oven and cook for 15 - 18 minutes or until cooked throughout.

For the Sauce

- Gently heat the cream in a heavy bottomed saucepan over a low heat, add the lemon juice, lemon spice, black pepper, garlic and mix well. Heat for 3 - 4 minutes or until the sauce begins to thicken - do not boil.

- Add the butter and stir until melted, serve immediately.

Serve with steamed asparagus or mangetout with creamy risotto.

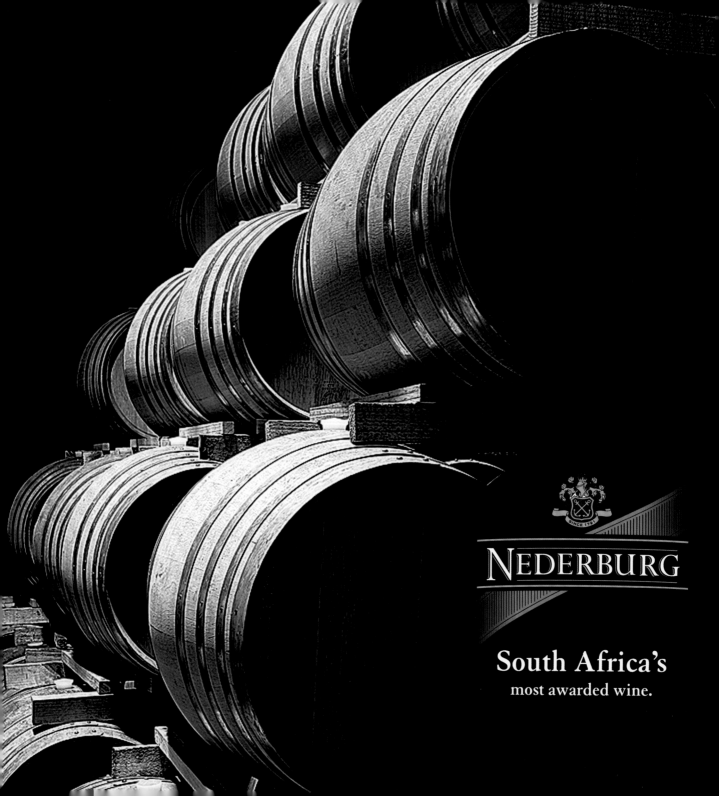

NEDERBURG

South Africa's
most awarded wine.

About Nederburg Wines...

South Africa's
most awarded wine.

Tradition and talent blend with passion, precision and patience at Nederburg, where classically structured wines are made with vibrant fruit flavours. Nederburg's hallmark combination of fruit and finesse continues to be rewarded around the world. The winery was awarded the trophy for the most successful producer on the Old Mutual Trophy Wine Show in both 2009 and 2008, and produced the winning Shiraz in the 2009 Syrah du Monde in France, as well as in the 2008 Lexus WINE Shiraz Challenge. Nederburg is frequently honoured in the Tri-Nations Wine Challenge, involving New Zealand and Australia. It also performs extremely well at the annual Veritas Awards (in 2009 winning the second highest number of double gold and gold medals), as well as the Michelangelo International Wine Awards. It has earned trophies, gold medals and best-in-class ratings on the annual International Wine & Spirit Competition in London, bringing home two trophies in 2009. Two of the cellar's wines are also rated five stars in the 2010 edition of the Platter's South African Wine guide. These are just some of the many accolades earned by Nederburg where hand-crafted, micro-cuvées for specialist winelovers and beautifully balanced and accessible wines for everyday enjoyment are made with equal commitment.

Nederburg is exported to key global markets in the UK, Europe, North America and Australasia, where it is steadily building a presence and reputation for elegantly styled wines with fruit-rich flavours. Its growing success is the result of an extensive infrastructure that includes ongoing viticultural research, implementation of pioneering vineyard practices, sourcing of top-quality grapes; major investment in cellar facilities and an international marketing and distribution network.

Razvan Macici heads the team as Nederburg cellarmaster. He is supported by two winemakers who work closely under his direction. They are Wilhelm Pienaar, who produces the red wines and Tariro Masayiti, who makes the whites.

Cabernet Sauvignon

Colour Dark ruby

Bouquet Aromas of blackcurrant, cassis, chocolate and mocha

Palate Ripe blackberry and currant, mocha and a hint of oak spices with firm, but supple tannins

Foods Excellent served with rosemary-infused lamb, petit poussin with thyme, seared AAA rump, fillet or sirloin, or Châteaubriand

Cabernet Sauvignon Rosé

Colour Lemon-green

Bouquet Grassy with citrus and stone fruit flavours

Palate A medium-bodied wine with a well-rounded mouth-feel and a soft, but long finish

Foods Excellent served with smoked salmon, risotto, summer salads or vegetarian dishes.

Chardonnay

Colour Vivacious green and gold

Bouquet Floral and fruit notes

Palate An inviting floral bouquet and a mélange of crisp lemon and pineapple flavours

Foods Excellent served with Thai and other oriental dishes as well as smoked salmon, grilled fish and cream sauces

Chardonnay / Viognier

Colour Straw

Bouquet An abundance of butterscotch and stone fruit with floral notes

Palate A medium-bodied wine with a lovely freshness and sweet fruit on the palate

Foods Excellent served with seafood, fish, poultry or veal dishes.

Merlot

Colour Dark ruby

Bouquet Soft rich fruit with strawberry and blackcurrent

Palate Medium bodied with attractive up-front fruit and a soft silky texture. with a soft Silky mouthfeel

Foods The winemaker suggests serving this wine with oxtail, casseroles, red meat, game, pizza and pasta.

Noble Late Harvest

Colour Bright yellow with hints of gold

Bouquet Aromas of dried peaches, apricot and honey, supported by spicy background notes

Palate Perfectly balanced sugar/acid ratio with dried fruit and vanilla spice and a lively acidity

Foods Excellent served with tomato soup, cakes, pastries, tarts and blue cheese

Pinotage

Colour   Deep red

Bouquet Plum and cherry aromas with slight oak spices in the background.

Palate   Well-balanced, rich fruit flavours with soft tannins and a lingering finish.

Foods   Excellent served with pasta, pizza, roast lamb, bobotie or chocolate.

Rosé

Colour   Pale rose

Bouquet Aromas of strawberries, ripe berries and dried herbs

Palate   Clean, fruity and refreshing flavours with a good acid structure

Foods   Excellent served with smoked salmon, summer salads or vegetarian dishes

Sauvignon Blanc

Colour   Lemon-green

Bouquet Grassy with citrus and tropical fruit flavours

Palate   A refreshing, medium-bodied wine with fresh aromas and a suitable finish

Foods   Excellent served with light meals seafood and salad

Sauvignon Blanc Chardonnay

Colour   Lemon-green

Bouquet Grassy with citrus and stone fruit flavours

Palate   A medium-bodied wine with a well-rounded mouth-feel and a soft, but long finish

Foods   Excellent served with seafood, fish, chicken and veal casseroles and cream based dishes.

Shiraz / Pinotage

Colour   Ruby with purple edges

Bouquet An abundance of ripe berries and spicy background aromas

Palate   Medium- to full-bodied with soft, velvety fruit, a hint of cinnamon and integrated oak flavours

Foods   Excellent served with Mediterranean meat dishes such as spicy lamb, souvlaki, kebabs or traditional roasts, oxtail and barbecued steaks

Stein

Colour   Straw yellow with green flecks

Bouquet Aromas of white peach, guava and raisins

Palate   Crisp and fresh with an abundance of ripe fruit flavours

Foods   Excellent served with pork, or Asian dishes, mild curries, liver pâté or baked puddings

Peri Peri Tiger Prawns

2-4 people - preparation 30 minutes (2h marinating) - cooking 6 - 12 minutes

Peri Peri refers to the African Bird's Eye chilli which commonly grows along the east coast of South Africa. My young nephew even found some growing is his back garden, although he thought they were juicy berries.

20	*large tiger prawns or langoustines*
4	*wooden skewers*
200ml	*peri peri marinade see pg 91*

- Remove head, legs and shell from the prawns.

- Marinate the prawns in peri peri sauce for between 2 and 24 hours.

- Soak the skewers in water for 30 minutes, this will prevent them from burning.

- Spike five tiger prawns on each of the skewers.

- Cook over suitable coals for 3 - 4 minutes each side or until firm and pink.

Alternatively:

- Place into 180°C / 350°F preheated oven for 10 - 12 mins, or until firm and pink

Serve with dressed leaves or rice with extra peri peri sauce.

Spinach & Goats' Cheese Chicken

2 people - preparation 20 minutes - cooking 12 - 15 minutes

Goats are very much a part of South Africa especially in rural communities where they are an essential part of many farms and villages. Goats' cheese is smooth and creamy and works well with the sweet mild taste of the succulent baby spinach .

2	chicken breast, skinless & boneless
60g	baby spinach - washed
1Tbl	water
1	garlic clove - minced
20g	goats' cheese
10	sundried tomatoes in oil (optional)
	salt & pepper

- Place the chicken breasts between two sheets of plastic wrap and gently pound with a rolling pin or meat mallot until the chicken is uniformly flattened to approx 5 - 6 mm / ¼ inch.

- Place the spinach in a small saucepan with the water, over a low to medium heat, cover and allow the spinach to wilt, approximately 2 minutes.

- Add the garlic, goats' cheese and sundried tomatoes to the spinach; melt the cheese and mix it well with the spinach and garlic over a low to medium heat until cheese has melted.

- Remove the top piece of plastic wrap from the chicken and evenly spread the spinach mix over the chicken breasts leaving approximately 2 ½ cm / 1 inch clear at the edge of the breast.

- Using the lower piece of plastic wrap carefully roll each breast and secure with two or three cocktail sticks. Discard the plastic wrap.

- Heat the olive oil in a frying pan over a medium heat, season the chicken and place in the pan and cook until golden brown on all sides for 12 - 15 minutes.

Serve with roast vine tomatoes and baby potatoes or salad see pg87.

Spiced Chicken

4 people - preparation 5 minutes - cooking 30 - 40 minutes

This simple but very tasty recipe is a firm family favourite and was kindly given to me by my sister-in-law. The fusion of the different spices gives incredible flavour and colour to the chicken.

4	large chicken breast	½tsp	salt
30ml	olive oil	¼tsp	pepper
3tsp	ground paprika	¼tsp	mixed spice
I tsp	curry powder (medium)	pinch	ground cayenne pepper
I tsp	ground cumin	I	garlic clove - minced
I tsp	ground coriander		

• Pat dry the chicken breasts with kitchen paper and place in a suitable mixing bowl

• Drizzle over the olive oil and rub it into the chicken

• Combine the spices and garlic, sprinkle over and rub into the chicken ensuring an even coating, allow to marinate for between 2 and 24 hours

• Place on a greased baking tray in 180°C / 350°F preheated oven, and cook for 30 - 40 minutes or until cooked throughout.

Alternatively

• Braai/barbecue for 15 - 20 minutes or until cooked throughout, turn occasionally.

Serve hot or cold with savoury rice or fresh pineapple salad see pg 87.

Beer Can Chicken

4-6 people - preparation 15-20 minutes (2h marinating) - cooking 2 hours 50 minutes

This modern addition to South African Cuisine has been widely embraced throughout the country as a great way to cook roast chicken. The use of a can of beer may sound odd but its inclusion is of great benefit as it provides a source of moisture and subtle flavour that results in succulent chicken.

I	small / medium chicken	½tsp	mixed spice
3	garlic clove - minced	pinch	cayenne pepper
3tsp	ground paprika	2tsp	rosemary - chopped
2tsp	curry powder (medium)	I tsp	thyme - chopped
2tsp	ground cumin	30ml	olive oil
2tsp	ground coriander	I	can of beer
I tsp	salt	I	medium onion
½tsp	pepper		

- Remove the neck and giblets and wash the chicken under cold water then dry the outside of the chicken

- Prepare the rub for the chicken by combining 2 garlic, paprika, curry, cumin, coriander, salt, pepper, mixed spice, cayenne, I tsp rosemary and thyme.

- Rub the olive oil and then the spice mix onto the chicken ensuring a full and even covering. If possible leave the chicken in a fridge for between 2 and 24 hours to allow the spices to infuse with the chicken.

- Open a can of your favourite beer, drink or remove half of the beer from the can. Add I tsp of rosemary and clove of crushed garlic to the can.

- Place the beer can on a flat service and slide the chicken over the top of the can until the can is secure in the cavity, use the two legs along with the can to steady the chicken. To improve the moistness of the meat, place the whole onion into the neck of the chicken above the beer can.

- Place the chicken with the can onto the braai/barbecue grill, you may need to use a small baking tray, over medium indirect heat and cover with the lid. Cook the chicken for 2 hours or until juices run clear when meat is spiked with a fork.

Alternatively:

- Place the chicken onto a suitable baking tray and place into 180°C / 350°F preheated oven. Cook the chicken for approximately 5 minutes to I hour or until juices run clear when meat is spiked with a fork.

Carefully remove the can as the liquid will be very hot.

Serve with salad see pg87 or chakalaka see pg84

Peri Peri Crispy Chicken

4-6 people - preparation 15-20 minutes (2h marinating) - cooking 15 - 20 minutes

This fiery little chilli is used throughout South Africa and now the world and has been developed beyond its original use as a sauce to include chilli rubs, salts and oils

4	*chicken breasts - large*
200ml	*Peri peri sauce see page 91*
200g	*flour*

- Trim excess fat from the chicken and cut into long finger wide strips.

- Marinate the chicken in peri peri for between 2 and 24 hours.

- Toss the chicken in the flour, ensuring full and even covering.

- Heat a frying pan or skillet over medium heat with about 5 - 6mm / ¼ inch deep of sunflower oil.

- Carefully place the chicken into the oil and cook for 2 - 3 minutes on each side or until golden brown (cook one piece first to ensure correct temperature and thorough cooking)

- Remove from the heat and place on kitchen paper to remove excess oil.

    Serve with chunky cut chips or fresh salad see pg87 and peri peri dipping sauce see pg75.

Cape Malay Chicken Curry

4-6 people - preparation 15-20 minutes (2h marinating) - cooking 50min - 2 hours

The Cape Malay also known as Cape Muslim community were originally brought to the Western Cape as slaves by The Dutch East India Company from the region of South East Asia.
They brought with them their own style of cooking, including the use of mild spices and fruits which has undoubtedly had a positive influence on South African cuisine.

2	medium onions - sliced		2	garlic cloves - minced
4Tbl	canola or olive oil		1 tsp	ginger - minced
2tsp	curry powder (medium)		50g	dried apricots - chopped
2tsp	ground cumin		100g	apricot or mango chutney
1 tsp	ground paprika		400g	chicken breast - cubed
1 tsp	ground cinnamon		400g	tomatoes - chopped
1 tsp	sugar		350ml	chicken stock
½tsp	ground turmeric		2	bay leaves
½tsp	salt		100g	green pepper - chopped
½tsp	pepper		2Tbl	coriander - chopped

- Saute onions in oil over medium heat until translucent.

- Mix the curry, cumin, paprika, cinnamon, sugar, turmeric, salt and pepper and mix with the onions over medium heat.

- Add garlic and ginger and mix well over medium heat.

- Reduce to low heat and add apricots and chutney.

- Stir in the chicken and tomatoes, mix well.

- Add stock and bay leaves, cover and simmer over low heat for 45 minutes, stirring occasionally.

- Add peppers and coriander, simmer for 15 minutes.

Garnish with fresh chopped coriander and serve with basmati rice and sambals pg 88.

Rooibos & Orange Duck

4 people - preparation 15 minutes - cooking 60 minutes

Rooibos or Redbush tea is unique to South Africa. The sweet flavour infused with fresh orange juice creates a tantalising sauce.

2	duck breasts
	salt & pepper
1 Tbl	olive oil

Orange & Rooibos sauce

300ml	fresh orange juice
1	rooibos tea bag
½tsp	cornflour
1 Tbl	caster sugar
½tsp	water
pinch	salt & pepper

- Score the skin side of the duck with a sharp knife, forming crossed lines, and season with salt and pepper.
- Heat the olive oil in a frying pan, when smoking hot place the duck into the pan, skin side down, and sear for 5 - 6 minutes or until the skin is golden brown.
- Remove from the heat and place the duck on a baking tray or oven dish and cook in 180°C / 350°F preheated oven for 6 - 7 minutes. If you prefer your duck 'well done' cook for a further 4 - 5 minutes.
- Remove from the oven and 'rest' for a few minutes.
- Slice the duck into thick strips and serve.

Sauce

- Place the orange juice and tea bag into a small saucepan and bring to the boil.
- Reduce heat and simmer for 3 - 4 minutes and then remove the tea bag.
- Mix the cornflour and water then add it to the orange juice while stirring
- Add sugar, salt and pepper, gently boil over medium to low heat until the liquid has reduced by two thirds and thickened.

Serve with stir fried vegetables or salad see pg87

Sun-blushed Tomato Pasta

2 people - preparation 10 minutes - cooking 15 - 20 minutes

South Africa has a significant number of post-colonial Italian immigrants who have helped to incorporate an Italian influence on the cuisine. This simple recipe combines common South African ingredients to create a satisfying pasta dish full of flavour.

200g	pasta (of your liking)	½	ripe avocado - peeled & finely chopped
800ml	water	14	sundried tomatoes in oil
¼t	salt	1/4tsp	salt
Sauce		1/4tsp	pepper
30g	onion - finely chopped	200ml	double cream
15g	butter	75g	soft goats' cheese
3T	white wine	40g	baby spinach
½	garlic clove - minced		

- Place the pasta in a suitable saucepan along with the water and salt, bring to the boil then reduce to low heat, cover and simmer for 10 - 15 minutes until pasta is just tender or 'al dente'

- Remove from the heat and strain

Sauce

- In a heavy bottomed saucepan, sauté the onion in 10g butter over med to high heat until translucent, add the wine, garlic, avocado and sundried tomatoes and reduce to low heat.

- Add salt, pepper and cream and simmer for 2 - 3 minutes.

- Crumble the soft goats' cheese into the cream and allow to melt stirring occasionally.

- Fold in the pasta and spinach and simmer for 2 - 3 minutes or until the spinach has wilted then add 5g butter and allow to melt.

Serve hot with fresh baked garlic bread

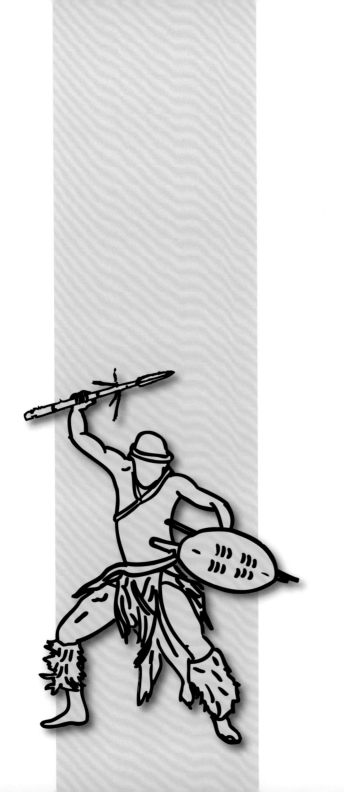

Sides & Sauces

Chakalaka

4 people - preparation 15 minutes - cooking 15 - 20 minutes

1 ½	medium onion - sliced
3	hot chillies - chopped
3Tbl	olive oil
1 Tbl	garlic - minced
1 Tbl	curry powder (medium)
1 Tbl	ground cumin
1 Tbl	cayenne pepper (optional, only if you really like it hot)
1 tsp	brown sugar

50g	cabbage - grated
50g	carrot - grated
50g	red bell pepper - chopped or sliced
50g	green bell pepper - chopped or sliced
400g	tomatoes - chopped
1 Tin	baked beans (optional)
	salt & pepper

- Sauté onions and chillies in the olive oil.

- Add garlic, curry, cumin, cayenne and sugar mixing well.

- Stir in the cabbage, carrots and peppers and reduce to a low heat.

- Introduce the tomatoes, mix well.

- Simmer for 10 - 15 minutes, if you want your chakalaka softer and more sauce like simmer for longer.

- Baked beans are often added and cooked into the chakalaka a few minutes before serving.

- Season to taste.

Butternut Potato Mash

4 people - preparation 10 - 15 minutes - cooking 15 - 25 minutes

Mashed butternut on its own is fantastic. This recipe softens the sweetness of the butternut and gives the mash a firmer texture.

750g	potatoes - washed & peeled	100ml	milk
250g	butternut squash - washed and peeled	50g	butter
pinch	salt		salt & pepper

- Cut the potatoes and butternut into even sized chunks and place in a saucepan of cold water with a little salt and bring to the boil, reduce to low heat, cover and simmer for 15 - 20 minutes or until tender when skewered with a knife.

- Drain off excess water and pass through a ricer or use a potato masher.

- Combine the milk and butter in a small saucepan and gently heat until the butter is melted, mix with the mash and season to taste.

Yellow Rice

2 people - preparation 2-3 minutes - cooking 15 - 20 minutes

220g	basmati rice	30g	raisins
½tsp	salt	650ml	water
1tsp	ground turmeric	10g	butter
1Tbl	brown sugar		
½tsp	ground cinnamon or half cinnamon stick		

- Combine the rice, salt, turmeric, sugar, cinnamon, raisins and water and bring to the boil in a heavy bottomed saucepan, reduce to low heat, cover and simmer for 10 – 12 minutes.

- Place the rice in a colander and rinse with boiling water.

- Add the butter and fluff with a fork, serve immediately.

Salad

2 - 4 people - preparation 10 minutes

Avocado & Strawberry Salad

200g	mixed lettuce leaves
1	avocado - peeled & sliced
12	strawberries - quartered
20g	pine nuts, pumpkin or mixed seeds
½	red onion - sliced
	balsamic reduction see pg 91

Pineapple Salad

200g	mixed lettuce leaves
100g	pineapple - chopped
100g	sweetcorn
50g	cucumber - diced
½	red onion - sliced
	honey mustard dressing see pg 91

- Rinse lettuce leaves with cold water and shake dry.

- Combine ingredients in a suitable mixing bowl.

- Finish with dressing.

- Serve as required.

Sambals

2 people - preparation 5 minutes

Originally introduced by Indonesian settlers as a hot chilli condiment it was firmly embraced as an essential accompaniment to curry. Nowadays the term Sambals in South Africa can cover anything from chopped dried fruit to fiery hot chilli sauce.

Tomato & Onion

50g	tomatoes - chopped
50g	white onion - chopped
I tsp	white vinegar
	salt & pepper

Combine and mix all the ingredients

Cucumber & Mint

I00g	cucumber
I Tbl	mint - chopped
I tsp	white vinegar
	salt & pepper

Combine and mix all the ingredients

Chilli & Coriander

I	red chilli - chopped
50g	white onion - chopped
40g	green bell better - chopped
5g	coriander - chopped
I tsp	white vinegar
	salt & pepper

Combine and mix all the ingredients

Banana & Coconut

I	banana
½tsp	lemon juice
2T	coconut - desiccated

Slice the banana into discs 5-6mm, place in a mixing bowl and drizzle over lemon juice the sprinkle over the coconut, toss the slices to ensure even coating

Sauces

Honey Mustard Salad Dressing

1 Tbl	wholegrain mustard
1 Tbl	Dijon mustard
2 Tbl	honey
2 Tbl	white wine vinegar or white wine
2 Tbl	olive oil / sunflower oil
1 tsp	orange juice
pinch	salt & pepper

Combine all ingredients in a mixing bowl and whisk by hand
makes approximately: 150ml

Sweet Peri Peri Sauce (hot)

2	African Bird's Eye Chiili - chopped (or adjust quantity to your liking)
125g	caster sugar
100ml	white vinegar
50ml	water
25ml	fresh lemon juice
½	red bell pepper - chopped
½	red onion - chopped
40g	tomato paste
2	garlic cloves - minced
3g	ginger - minced
1/2tsp	oregano - dried
1/4tsp	salt
1/4tsp	pepper

Combine all the ingredients and blend until smooth.
Place in small sauce pan and bring to the boil.
Reduce to low heat, cover and simmer for 20 – 30 minutes,
remove from heat and allow to cool.
makes approximately: 250ml

Lemon Pepper Dressing

50ml	olive oil
3 Tbl	lemon juice
1 Tbl	white wine vinegar
pinch	cracked black peppercorn
1/4tsp	salt
½tsp	lemon zest / rind

Combine the ingredients and blend for 30 - 45 seconds.
makes approximately: 110ml

Balsamic Reduction / Syrup

100ml	balsamic vinegar
100g	white caster sugar

Combine in a small pot. Bring to the boil and immediately
reduce to a low heat. Allow to simmer until liquid reduces by one
third. The balsamic reduction should evenly coat the back of a
spoon. Take care not to reduce the liquid too much or you will
caramelise the mixture.

Allow to cool and use as a dressing for salads, breads, meats
and more.
makes approximately: 120ml

Durban, South Africa

KwaZulu-Natal & Durban

Having lived in Hillcrest just outside the city of Durban and with my family still living in Westville I always start and finish any time in South Africa with Kwa-Zulu Natal.

KwaZulu-Natal is the home of the Zulu Kingdom, the largest ethnic group in South Africa. The Zulus, who rose to greatness under the leadership of King Shaka in the late 1700's, famously battled against the British in the late 1800's with nothing more than shields and spears. Located a short distance from Durban outside Hillcrest in The Valley of A Thousand Hills is a living Zulu museum where local Zulus dressed in traditional attire provide an entertaining introduction to Zulu culture and dancing to visitors from all over the world. The stunning landscape of the valley of 1000 hills lies at its peak at Botha's Hill from here you can look out over the valley or even the Indian Ocean. The valley of a thousand hills has been carved out over the centuries by the water flowing down from the distant Drakensberg Mountain Range. The Drakensberg is the highest mountain range in South Africa and as a World Heritage Site it also boasts the largest collection of bush cave paintings in the world, approximately 35-40,000 drawings

Throughout Kwa-Zulu Natal you will find yourself spoilt for choice when it comes to entertainment, activities and shopping. The opportunities for thrills are as vast as the land itself from zip lining through tree top canopies to paint-balling in the bush, white water rafting to spotting the 'Big Five' in one of the many luxurious safari parks. For those who prefer something less adventurous the availability of impressive shopping malls will keep you entertained for hours if not days at a time.

Durban or Thekwini "the place where the earth and the ocean meet"

Durban, a sub-tropical cosmopolitan city located in KwaZulu-Natal on the east coast of South Africa, is often referred to as 'South Africa's Playground' and is the third largest city in South Africa. Durban is home to South Africa's busiest port which makes it a popular location for business and conferencing events. However its main appeal for tourists and family holiday makers is the climate and beachfront. Also known as the 'Golden Mile' this stretch of beach is popular with locals for swimming and of course surfing, next to the beach are other attractions including craft markets, gardens and a replica model city of Durban. Further along the coast at South Beach is one of the world's largest aquariums, Ushaka Marine World, this venue with its nautical themed aquarium and water park is popular all year round. I have visited the aquarium and water park many times and it never fails to impress me.

Pietermaritzburg or Maritzburg, affectionately referred to by the locals as 'The last Outpost of The British Empire', is the capital city of Kwa-Zulu Natal. Although originally founded by the Voortrekkers, Dutch/Afrikaner pioneers from the Cape Colony, it was subsequently developed by the British in the late 1800's and to this day maintains a British 'feel' with its Victorian and Edwardian style architecture. As a city it is full of charm and character with a wide variety of shops, restaurants and hotels ideal for a day trip visit or an extended break. Piertmaritzburg is also an ideal gateway to the Kwa-Zulu Natal midlands, the Drakensberg and of course the wilderness with its many safari game resorts.

For something less challenging than the two big cities you can always travel along the Coast taking in some of the Coastal towns such as Amanzimtoti, Ballito and Umhlanga Rocks. These coastal locations are ideal for swimming, snorkelling and scuba diving but for those land lovers among us you can simply 'park off' (relax) and soak up the sunshine, unless you would prefer a round of golf, some shopping or a fantastic meal. This coastline of golden beaches, rocky coves, lagoons and the warm Indian Ocean makes Kwa-Zulu Natal a popular destination all year round.

Desserts & Drinks

Melk Tert

8 - 10 people - preparation 10 - 15 minutes - cooking 5 - 10 minutes

Melk Tert or Milk Tart could arguably be described as the national dessert of South Africa. Like any popular dish there are different methods of preparation. However you can be sure that any good Melk Tert will be light, fluffy and dusted with cinnamon.

Pastry	
130g	caster sugar
115g	butter - cubed
1	egg - beaten
225g	plain flour

Filling	
1 Tbl	flour
½ T	cornflour
120g	sugar
1	egg
½ tsp	vanilla extract
500ml	milk
30g	butter

Pastry
- In a mixing bowl combine the sugar and butter, mix together, add the egg and cream into a paste.
- Sieve the flour and baking powder together and add to the butter, gently crumble together, to form a dough, be careful not to over handle as the butter will melt.
- Press the pastry into a well greased flan ring or pie dish approx. 25cm in diameter ensuring an even lining, refrigerate for 15 – 20 minutes.
- Line the inside of the pastry with baking foil or greaseproof paper and fill with dried peas, lentils or similar.
- Place in 180°C/350°F preheated oven and bake for 10 - 12 minutes, remove from the oven then remove the peas and lining. Return to oven for 2 - 3 minutes.
- Remove from oven and allow to cool

The Filling
- Combine the flour, cornflour and sugar in a mixing bowl.
- Beat the egg and vanilla together and add to the flour and mix into a smooth paste.
- Bring the milk and butter to the boil in a heavy bottomed saucepan then reduce to a low to medium heat.
- Add the paste to the milk stirring continuously until the mix begins to thicken.
- Remove from the heat and pour into the base.
- Sprinkle with cinnamon powder and refrigerate for between 1 and 2 hours.

Great served as a main dessert or with a cup of coffee

Cocoa Cola Cake

12 portions - preparation 15 minutes - cooking 50 - 60 minutes

A family recipe passed on to me by my sister-in-law this is sure to please anyone who favours a rich moist chocolate dessert. This cake is best served hot from the oven but I can assure you it is great cold or reheated for breakfast lunch and dinner.

250g	plain flour
375g	caster sugar
250g	butter
3Tbl	cocoa powder
240ml	Coca-Cola
2	eggs
125ml	butter milk
1 Tbl	vanilla essence
1 tsp	baking soda

Icing

125g	butter
3 Tbl	Coca-Cola
½ Tbl	cocoa powder
180g	icing sugar

- Sieve flour and combine with sugar.

- Heat butter, cocoa and Coca-Cola until boiling and pour over flour and sugar, beat for 2 min.

- Beat the eggs, buttermilk, vanilla and baking soda together and add to the above.

- Bake at 180°C / 350°F in preheated oven for 50 – 60 min.

For the Icing

- Melt butter in a saucepan and then stir in rest of ingredients until thickened.

- Pour over warm cake immediately.

Serve warm with fresh cream or ice cream.

Malva Pudding

6-8 portions - preparation 15 minutes - cooking 45 - 50 minutes

This sweet apricot sponge pudding is originally of Dutch origin and has developed into one of South Africas' top favourite desserts. Excellent served both hot and cold especially with vanilla pod ice cream or a simple custard.

3	eggs - medium		360g	plain flour
300g	caster sugar		*Sauce:*	
30ml	apricot jam		225ml	cream
35g	butter		120g	butter
1 ½tsp	white vinegar		120g	caster sugar
150ml	milk		120ml	milk
1 ½tsp	baking powder		½tsp	vanilla essence

- Whisk the eggs and beat into caster sugar until smooth, add apricot jam and beat together.

- Melt the butter and combine with vinegar and milk, add to egg and sugar mix, beat together.

- Combine the baking powder and flour and sift into a bowl, add to the mix a third at a time, ensuring thorough mixing. Beat until smooth.

- Spoon the mixture into a greased baking dish 20cm x 26cm and cover with kitchen foil. Place in a preheated oven, 180°C / 350°F, for 45 - 50 mins. Spike with a skewer or knife in the middle to check it is fully baked.

Sauce

- Mix all the ingredients and heat over a medium to low heat

- Malva pudding is best served warm from the oven. Gently spike the surface of the pudding with a fork, pour over the sauce and allow it to soak into the pudding.

Portion and serve with vanilla ice cream or custard.

Amarula Chocolate Brownies

12 portions - preparation 15 minutes - cooking 20 - 25 minutes

Amarula liqueur is made from the fruit of the Marula tree. The sweet and creamy flavour works perfectly with the rich flavour of chocolate.

100g	butter	3	eggs - medium
50g	dark chocolate	50ml	Amarula liqueur
50g	cocoa powder	100g	chocolate pieces / chunks
30g	plain flour		
½tsp	baking powder		
175g	caster sugar		

- Melt butter and dark chocolate in a bowl over a pot of hot water.

- Mix cocoa, flour, baking powder and sugar add to melted chocolate.

- Beat eggs and add to chocolate along with Amarula.

- Add 75g of the chocolate pieces to the mix.

- Spoon mixture into a greased baking tray approximately 20cm x 26cm.

- Sprinkle remaining chocolate pieces on top and bake in 180°C / 350°F preheated oven for 20-25mins. Brownies should still be a little wet in the middle when you remove from the oven as they will continue to cook for a few minutes after.

- Allow to cool and tip out of baking tray and cut into 12 individual pieces.

  Great with coffee or as a dessert served with ice-cream, strawberries and chocolate sauce.

Sweet Peppermint Tart

8-10 people - preparation 30 minutes

This rich and flavoursome dessert is a modern South African favourite. Usually made with a variety of South African products I have adapted this great dish to include more locally available ingredients.

250ml	whipping cream	100g	mint Aero or mint match makers or mint crisp chocolate - grated
2 - 3 drops	peppermint essence	1 ½ packets	'nice' biscuits - crushed
397g	caramel condensed milk		

- Whip the cream until stiff.

- Add essence and condensed milk and 75g of mint aero to the whipped cream and mix well.

- Place a layer of biscuits in the bottom of a buttered dish approximately 20cm x 26cm.

- Spoon a third of the cream mix over the biscuits, spreading evenly.

- Continue in layers leaving a thick layer of cream on top.

- Scatter the remaining grated Aero over the top and refrigerate for 2 - 3 hours.

Serve with fresh cream or ice-cream and fresh mint.

Koeksisters

18 servings - preparation 20 minutes (1 - 2 hours refrigerating) - cooking 15 - 20 minutes

These braided doughnut like fritters are coated in sweet sticky syrup and are popular throughout South Africa. This recipe is based on that of the Afrikaner tradition of making it as a sweet doughy fritter rather than the more cake like, spicier version of the Cape Malay community.

<u>Dough</u>			<u>Syrup</u>	
240g	self raising flour		400g	caster sugar
½tsp	salt		240ml	water
25g	butter		pinch	salt
I	egg		I Tbl	lemon juice
50ml	milk		I	cinnamon stick
			¼tsp	vanilla extract

Syrup:
*   Combine the sugar, water, salt, lemon juice, cinnamon stick and vanilla extract in a saucepan and bring to the boil.
*   Reduce to a low to medium heat and simmer for 8 - 10minutes or until the liquid thickens like a syrup allow to cool.

Dough:
*   Combine the flour and salt and sieve together into mixing bowl.
*   Cut the butter into small cubes and gently rub into the flour, do not over handle.
*   Beat the egg and combine it with the milk.
*   Introduce the milk to the flour a third at a time and fold together, be careful not to over knead the dough.
*   Alternatively use a food mixer or ready made pastry.
*   Refrigerate the dough for 1 - 2 hours.
*   Place the dough on a smooth surface lightly dusted with flour.
*   Roll out the dough until it is approximately 5-6mm / ¼ inch thick.
*   Cut the dough into even strips approximately 8cm x 2cm.
*   Keeping a join at one end cut each strip lengthwise into three - see diagram.
*   Platt or braid each piece of dough, ensuring you pinch the end to stop it falling apart while cooking.
*   Add the sunflower oil to a frying pan or skillet, the oil should be at least 5 - 6mm / ¼ inch deep, heat over medium heat.
*   Place one pastry into the oil and cook until golden brown, turn and cook until golden brown all over. N.B. If the oil is too hot the pastry will brown on the outside but the inside will remain doughy inside.
*   Remove from the oil and submerge the pastry in the syrup for 20 - 30 seconds to absorb the syrup. Place the pastry on a wire rack, to cool, allowing excess syrup to drip away from the pastry.

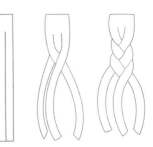

Great as a sweet treat or dessert.

Rooibos & Lemon Jelly

4 - 6 people - preparation 10 minutes

Rooibos or 'red bush' tea has been a favourite in South Africa for many generations and is now becoming popular throughout the world. Rooibos has high levels of antioxidants which makes it a popular herbal tea.

4	small sheets gelatine 7cm x 11cm
600ml	water
4	rooibos tea bags
120g	caster sugar
2Tbl	lemon juice

- Soak the gelatine sheets in 30ml of water for 4 - 5 minutes.

- Add the Rooibos tea to the remaining water (570ml) and bring to the boil, reduce heat and simmer for 3 - 4 minutes.

- Remove the tea bags and stir in the sugar and lemon juice.

- Lift the gelatine out of the water and squeeze out excess liquid, add to the tea and stir until melted over a low heat, do not boil.

- Remove from the heat and pour into a suitable jelly mould or wine glasses and allow to cool for 30minutes. Place in refrigerator and chill for 2 - 3hours.

Serve with vanilla ice-cream or Chantilly cream.

Don Pedro

1 Person - preparation 5 minutes

When in South Africa there is nothing better than watching the sun set with a 'sundowner'. This tradition to enjoy an alcoholic beverage with friends and family at sun down is common with many a South African. This recipe is great as a sun downer or as an evening dessert drink combining the fresh flavour of vanilla with the distinct flavour of Amarula or a similar spirit of your choice.

30ml	*Amarula, Scotch whiskey or Kahlua*
1-2 scoop	*vanilla icecream*
50-60ml	*double cream*
¼ tsp	*chocolate - grated*

- Combine the ingredients in a blender and blend until smooth.

- Serve in a champagne flute or wine glass garnished with grated chocolate.

- For extra presentation I like to drizzle a little chocolate sauce into the glass before pouring in the Don Pedro.

Great to drink anytime.

Nambiti Frozen Yoghurt

8 people - preparation 10 minutes - freezing 2 - 3 hours

*This recipe was given to me by the chef at **Elephant Rock Lodge** in Nambiti Game Reserve in South Africa. This charming boutique safari lodge offers luxurious accommodation and service with fantastic meals and unforgettable game viewing experiences.*

500g	*fruit yoghurt*
397g	*condensed milk*
240ml	*cream*

• Mix yoghurt and condensed milk together in suitable bowl.

• Whip the cream to a soft peak and gently fold into the yoghurt mix.

• Pour into 8 small ramekins, small cups or tupperware dishes.

• Cover and place on a flat surface in the freezer and freeze for 2 - 3 hours.

Serve with fresh cherries.

Amarula Liqueur Coffee

1 person - preparation 5 minutes

Liqueur coffees are popular all over the world and are made with any number of different liqueurs. This recipe brings together the unique fruity flavour of the award winning Amarula liqueur with the bold taste of fresh coffee.

30ml	*Amarula*
1 shot (30ml)	*espresso*
	boiling water
	whipped cream
	chocolate - grated

- Combine the Amarula and espresso in a latte glass or Irish coffee glass.

- Add boiling water.

- Top off with whipped cream.

- Garnish with grated chocolate

Great as an after dinner drink.

Index